D1508601

# CATS

Franklin Watts
8 Cork Street
London W1

Copyright © 1980 Franklin Watts Limited

SBN 85166 811 9

U.S. edition SBN: 531–04119–0
Library of Congress Catalog
Card No. 79–57273

Thanks are due to the following for their help with
the photography of this book:
Marianne Abrahart; Pedigree Pet Foods Education
Centre; James Ramsay, Linda and Peter Wilton

Printed in Great Britain by
Tindal Press, Chelmsford, Essex

# Junior Petkeeper's Library

# CATS

by
FIONA HENRIE

CONSULTANT EDITOR:
MICHAEL FINDLAY, M.R.C.V.S.

Photographs by Marc Henrie

FRANKLIN WATTS
London/New York/Sydney/Toronto/1980

# Contents

# ntroduction

A cat is a live animal—not a toy.

It has real feelings, just as people do.

It can feel hungry and thirsty, or full and contented.

It can feel frightened, or it can feel safe.

It can feel comfortable, or it can feel pain.

A cat needs to be cared for all the time.

It will cost you extra money to feed and look after your cat.

You will need to have your parents' permission to have a cat as you may need some help to look after it properly.

But you will find your pet a fascinating and beautiful creature which will give you and your family much pleasure.

NOTE TO PARENTS
Should you decide to add a cat to your family, please be absolutely certain that it is wanted, both by your child and your family, and that it will not be a passing fancy. You must be sure that you are willing to supervise its care and well-being for eleven or more years, and to bear the cost of its upkeep. It would be unfair to your child, to the cat, and to you and your family to become unwilling owners of a cat.

# Buying a Cat

Perhaps you know someone whose cat has
had a litter of kittens.

Maybe you could have one of the kittens
when it is old enough to leave its mother
—about seven to eight weeks of age.

Or you could get a cat from a breeder.

A breeder sells pedigreed cats and kittens.

Or you could give a home to a homeless
or stray cat through one of the animal
rescue agencies.

Never give, or receive, a cat or kitten as
a gift unless you are sure that it is
wanted and will be looked after all
its life.

Three well-looked after cats.
A pedigreed cat is one which is pure bred. Its parents and grand-parents have been of the same breed for several generations. A cross-bred cat is one whose parents are of different breeds.

# What to Look for

It is important to choose a healthy cat.

It should have clear, bright eyes, clean ears, nose and mouth, and a clean coat without any bare patches.

Kittens should be lively, playful and interested in everything around them.

Ask if you can see the mother of a kitten you like.

It is a good sign if she is healthy.

If you decide to have a pedigreed cat, go along to the breeder while the kittens are very young.

There you can choose which one you will have when it is old enough.

A non-pedigreed cat, or mongrel, is a cat whose parents are of no special breed, but mongrels can be just as beautiful and make just as good pets as pedigreed cats.

There are long-haired cats and there are short-haired cats.

Cat bed made of
basket weave.

Every cat should
have its own brush
and comb.

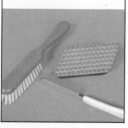

You will need some
small dishes or
bowls—for food,
milk and water.

Do not let the cat
or kitten out of
doors at first so get
a plastic litter box
for its toilet. Also
buy a bag of litter
or wood shavings
to put in the box.

# Preparing for your Cat

Before you collect your cat, it is important
to have ready all the things it will need.

Some things can be bought at a pet shop
and some can be made.

A cat needs its own bed to sleep in, with a
blanket or cushion for warmth.

You could choose a basket, a bed of rigid
plastic (very easy to keep clean), or a
soft bed covered with fabric.

You can even make a bed yourself from a
strong cardboard box.

You should buy enough food for the first
few days.

The basket should have plenty of air holes, and should be large enough for the cat to turn round in.

The cat may be frightened and try to get out of the carrier, so make sure that it is shut tightly. This is very important if you are in a car. If the cat jumps out of the carrier and disturbs the driver, it could cause an accident.

If you want to take your cat on a journey, you will need a special carrier box or basket.

Some are made of basket weave, and some of rigid plastic.

The basket or box should be strong, and have a tight cover.

If you want your cat to wear a collar, choose one made of soft leather, lined with felt.

A tag (with your name and address) can be fixed to the collar.

A bell on the collar helps to warn birds that a cat is around.

A cat collar must have an elastic part, so the cat can slip its head out if it gets stuck trying to pass through a narrow space. Without the elastic section, the cat could choke.

Some cats can be trained to wear a harness and walk with a lead or leash. The harness goes round the cat's body and the lead is clipped to the top.

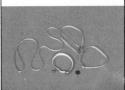

Make your journey as short as you can to keep the cat from being too upset. Some cats do not like car journeys, so do not worry if your cat is slightly sick.

# Taking your Cat Home

When you collect your cat or kitten take a strong box or carrier to put it in with a couple of sheets of newspaper inside.

Plastic carrying box.

A strong, dry cardboard box would do. Punch lots of air holes into the sides and top so that the cat can breathe.

Do not fill the box up with a fluffy cushion. This would take up all the space needed for the cat's body and make it hard for the cat to breathe.

Find out what the kitten or cat is used to eating, and how often to feed it, so that you can continue with the same food.

Ask for a piece of the cat's usual bedding to help your pet feel less strange in its new home.

A new cat or kitten may feel frightened. It may run away from you or try to hide under the furniture, especially if it is a stray or rescued cat.

# Settling in

Your new cat or kitten will feel a little strange in its new home for the first few days.

Be very patient and gentle with it.

Put the cat's bed in a quiet corner of the room where it will not be disturbed.

Put its food dishes where the cat will not be upset while it is eating.

Keep the cat in one room at first, so it can get used to its new surroundings gradually.

Put lots of newspaper on the floor around the cat's bed at night, in case it cannot get to the litter box in time.

Put the litter box well away from the bed and the food bowls.

A cat flap or cat door can be built into your own door or window for the cat to go in and out when it likes. All cats need to sharpen their claws. A scratching post will keep the cat from tearing the furniture and carpets.

When the kitten or cat has finished its food, throw away any leftovers and give fresh food at the next meal.

All cats need plenty of drinking water.
Change the water in the cat's dish every day, even if it has not been touched.
Not all cats like milk to drink so give both milk and water at first until you know which it likes.

Most cats eat grass, as it helps them digest their food. If you live where there is no grass, you can buy a plastic pot already planted with grass, and grow it on your window sill.

# Feeding

Kittens of six to twelve weeks need four small meals, evenly spaced through the day.

If you have to change what the kitten has been used to eating, do so gradually or you might upset its stomach.

Take the food dish away about five minutes after the kitten has finished eating, even if some food is left.

When the kitten is about three to four months old, give it three meals a day, with larger portions than before.

There should be fresh water always for your cat to drink.

Most canned foods provide everything your cat needs to keep it fit and healthy.
However, some pet keepers believe that there should be some fresh meat in a cat's diet.

Meat should be the main part of the diet of an adult cat.

Cut up the meat into small pieces with a little green vegetable or carrot, some small pieces of brown bread, or cereal mixed with gravy or water.

You can also give your cat meals of fish (if you take out the bones), cheese, eggs or sardines.

Some cats like to chew on a raw beef bone.

This helps to clean their teeth, and also gives them extra minerals.

Cats over seven months need 25 g of food for each kilogram (1½ oz per pound) of its own weight each day.

If your cat eats "dry" packaged cat food, it needs to drink more water.
If your cat does not drink very much, do not give it dry food at all, unless it is served moist.

Cleanliness is very important.
Make sure that all the cat's dishes are washed in hot water after every meal, separately from your own plates, and dried separately too.

Cat bed made of soft material.
It is not a good idea to let your cat sleep on your bed, as you could catch germs from it.

A cat lying stretched out or with its body in a curve, is not completely asleep. When it is curled right up in a ball with its tail wrapped tight round its nose, it is in a deep sleep.

Cats will choose a place in the sun or by the fire or the radiator to have a nap. Try to keep cats off the chairs as their hair can be very difficult to clean up.

# Sleeping

Your cat's bed should be in a place where it will not be disturbed.

It should be away from cold air.

Choose a suitable place as soon as you get your cat and always leave the bed in the same place.

Try to persuade the cat to sleep there—though you may find the cat will sleep wherever it wants to.

Little kittens, like human babies, need a lot of sleep.

When your kitten is sleeping or looks tired, let it sleep until it wakes up by itself.

Keep the litter box in the same place always so that the cat will know where to find it.

You can use wood shavings or torn-up newspaper as litter, but these might smell. Special cat litter, sold in bags, is far better. Cat litter also helps to keep down smells.

# Toilet Training

You can train your cat to go out of doors, or to use a litter box.

A litter, or toilet, box is a shallow box filled with absorbent material called litter.

Your kitten may have been taught by its mother to use a litter box.

Show the box to the cat as soon as it arrives—and always after it eats or drinks.

It will soon learn to go there by itself.

If you dabble its paws in the litter, it will quickly understand what it has to do.

Clean out the dirty parts of the litter as soon as you can after the cat has used the box.

A plastic scoop is useful for this job. When the litter is too soiled, change it completely, and wash and disinfect the tray thoroughly.

After this job it is very important that you wash your hands well with soap and hot water. Wash, too, after touching the cat, especially if you are going to eat anything.

Try to brush and comb your cat at about the same time each day.
This will make it easier for you to remember.
Take special care not to touch the cat's eyes, nose or mouth with the brush or comb.
These parts are very tender.

# Grooming

Brush your kitten with a very soft baby brush for just a few minutes each day.

When your cat is older, you will need a brush and comb to keep its coat in good condition.

Cats lick themselves all over.

This helps to keep their fur clean.

They will still need some help from you to remove the "dead" hair.

Otherwise they can swallow their fur, which causes fur balls in their stomachs.

Fur balls can make your cat sick—especially if it has long hair.

A healthy cat will always wash itself. This is called "self grooming". A cat which does not wash itself may be ill.

The mother cat washes her kittens from the time they are born until they are old enough to do it for themselves.

16

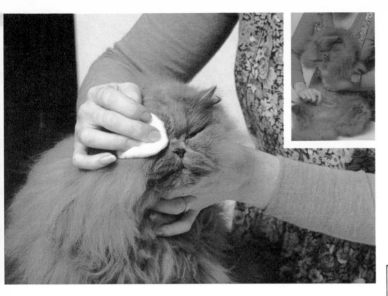

Try to get a grown-up to wipe round the eyes for you, or at least to hold the cat still. *(Inset)* Brushing helps to loosen dead hair; combing helps to lift it out.

Brush the cat all over first of all in the direction the fur grows, and then in the opposite direction.

Do not pull out tangled or matted parts with the comb, but work them out with your fingers.

Take special care around the ears and where the legs join the body as there may be tangles.

Sometimes you will need to clean just under the cat's eyes with pads of damp soft material.

Use a different piece for each side of the face and take care not to touch the eyes.

If your cat does not go out, its claws may grow rather long and need to be cut. This is a job for your vet or for a grown-up who knows how to do it.

Your kitten or cat may have fleas, small insects that live in the cat's fur and bite its skin. They are very irritating and will make the cat scratch a lot. Your vet will give you some powder or spray to put on the cat's coat to kill the fleas. It is important to get rid of them as they could make the cat ill.

Correct way of holding a cat.

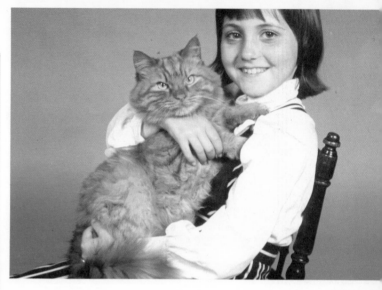

To pick up a kitten put one hand under its chest with your fingers between its front legs and your thumb on the outside of one front leg.
Slide the other hand underneath its bottom and lift.

Never pick up a kitten under its stomach alone or by its front legs. You could hurt it badly.

When cats are fully grown, they can jump up very high. They can balance and walk on very narrow ledges and fences. Kittens do not have the strength or the practice to do this.

# Handling

Kittens are very delicate, and can be hurt very easily.

Always pick them up gently, and hold them firmly—but not tightly—so that they feel safe.

Adult cats may be too heavy for you to pick up easily.

Unless you know the cat well, and you know the correct way to hold it, it is better not to try.

Never put a kitten on a place that is too high for it to have jumped there by itself.

Remember not to pull hard when a kitten (or cat) has a piece of string in its mouth or caught in its claws or you could hurt it.

# Toys

Cats can be very lively and kittens even more so.

They need exercise to help them grow strong and healthy.

Cats and kittens love to chase things.

Even a leaf or a piece of string will keep them amused.

Never give cats anything to play with that has sharp edges.

Do not give any toys which have been painted with lead paint.

Do not give anything so small that a cat could swallow it.

There are all sorts of toys sold specially for cats—soft toys, rubber toys and some with bells inside them.

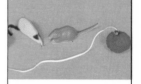

Never give an animal a plastic bag to play with. It might suffocate if its head became trapped inside.

Although they are very pretty, dried grasses could be a danger if they are dyed different shades. The dye could be poisonous to cats.

When you are boarding your cat in a strange place, take along its bed, brush and comb, and toys to remind it of home.

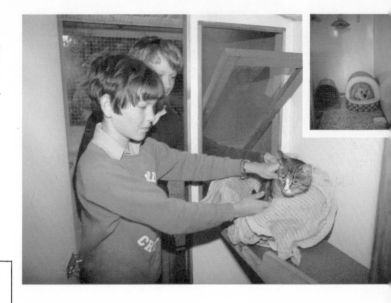

Each cat should have its own living area at the boarding place with a wired-in run in the open air.
Each pen should have a solid barrier, made of plastic, for example, or a gap of 46 cm (18 in) between it and the next one. This gap is sometimes called a sneeze barrier. It keeps germs from spreading.

Tell the people in charge what your cat likes to eat. Tell them about any medicines the cat needs, and anything else you can think of.

# Going Away

If you and your family are going away remember to find somone to care for your cat.

You could ask a friend or the person next door to come in to feed the cat and make sure that it is all right.

If there is no one to take care of the cat, you could take it to a place that boards pets.

You should arrange this early, as such places are busy at holiday times.

To board your cat you must provide an up-to-date vaccination certificate.

All animals entering Britain go to special quarantine kennels. They live there, separate from all the other animals, until the vet is sure they have not brought rabies with them.

At the kennels the animals are examined by a vet when they arrive. Then they are given a vaccination against rabies. The vet examines them again from time to time during the six months they are there. People who try to avoid leaving their pets in quarantine have to pay large fines.

# Quarantine

Rabies is a very dangerous disease which all mammals, including cats, dogs, monkeys — and human beings — can catch.

In most countries, including the U.S.A., where rabies exists, all pets are vaccinated against the disease.

Other countries, such as Britain, do not have rabies.

To stop rabies entering when animals go to Britain from abroad, the law says that cats must go into "quarantine" for six months.

A kittening box (right) is a special bed for the mother and her kittens. A heating lamp can help to keep the kittens warm.
The kittening box can be made from a packing case with a hole cut in the side for the mother to go in and out. The hole should be too high for the kittens to get out.

# Breeding

If your female cat runs free out of doors she should be neutered when she is five months old unless you want her to have kittens.

A male, or tom, cat should be neutered at five months of age, too.

Otherwise he will be father to many kittens from female cats in the area.

Also un-neutered tom cats may smell bad.

When the female is "in kitten" (pregnant) she will need special food.

She will eat more than usual and need extra vitamins and minerals.

If you have a pedigreed female cat and you want her to have kittens, she must be mated to a male of the same breed. Then her kittens will be the same breed, too. It is best to arrange this through a breeder.
You will need to take your certificate of pedigree to the breeder.

Kittens are born with their eyes closed and do not open them until they are seven to ten days old.
New-born kittens should not be handled.

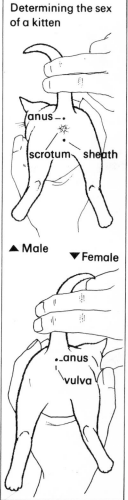

Determining the sex of a kitten

anus —
scrotum   sheath

▲ Male        ▼ Female

—anus
vulva

Kittens are born about nine weeks after mating.

When the kittens are born, their mother will wash them all over and feed them with her milk.

When kittens are three to four weeks old, they can start to lap milk from a saucer.

Gradually give them baby food, baby cereals and small pieces of meat.

By the time the kittens are five to six weeks old, two of their meals should be meat meals.

When they are six to eight weeks old, they should not need to drink from their mother at all.

There should be nothing around the room which could injure the kittens (such as electric wires which they could chew).

If there is a chimney it should be blocked up.
Even quite small kittens can climb curtains which reach the floor.
A large pen, like a child's play pen, can be a great help to keep the kittens in. (Of course, a pen with bars the kittens can get through, will be of no use.)

Kitten enjoying the sunshine.

# Kittens

At first the mother cat will keep her kittens clean by washing them all over.

Soon their eyes will open and they will move around.

Spread lots of newspapers on the floor until the kittens are toilet-trained.

The mother may take the kittens to the litter box, or you can do this.

It will not be long before they go on their own.

If there are lots of kittens, keep them in a room with linoleum or tiles on the floor.

These are much easier to keep clean than a carpet.

Young cats are very inquisitive and will go everywhere.

Give each kitten its own food dishes.

All the dishes must be absolutely clean and should be washed up as soon as the kittens have finished eating.

The mother will protect her kittens but she may not always be around when they get into trouble.

They run around the floor so fast that you can never be quite sure where they are, so be very careful where you step.

Cats and dogs are said to be natural enemies. But cats and dogs that live in the same house can get on very well together.

Kittens should be handled gently and carefully from a very early age.

Then they will be quite used to people by the time they are old enough to go to their new home.

When you have had the kitten or cat for about a week, make an appointment to take it to the vet for a general health examination.
If you have any questions about your cat's health or care, you can ask the vet or the nurse who may be helping.

The vet will examine your cat carefully.
The vet may ask you a few questions about your pet. Answer as carefully as you can.
Your vet may give your parents pills or medicine for the cat. The vet will tell your parents how and when to give them.
REMEMBER: Pills and medicine are not good to eat. *Never* take them yourself.

# Health Care

When you decide to have a cat, find out who your nearest vet is.

Write down the vet's name, address and telephone number.

Always take the cat to the vet if you are worried about its health.

Never try to treat it yourself.

Some signs of illness in your cat are:

- it does not eat for twenty-four hours;
- its eyes and nose are running, and it is sneezing;
- it is sick and has diarrhea.

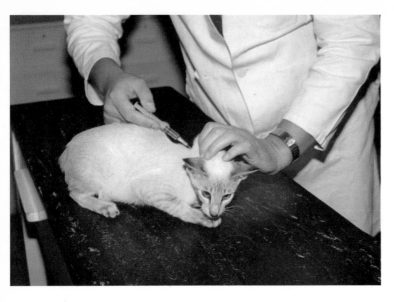

You will have to pay for the vaccinations but they are very worthwhile. They will protect your cat's health.
The vaccination injections (shots or jabs) do not hurt the cat.
When the full vaccination has been given, the vet will give you a certificate with the date on it.
You should keep this in a safe place.

There are two common diseases which cats can catch, called cat flu and feline enteritis.

Protect your cat against these diseases by asking your vet to vaccinate it.

Your kitten should be vaccinated when it is about three months old.

You may have to visit the vet twice for these injections.

The protection will last for at least a year.

Then you should take the cat for a booster injection.

Sometimes the cat flu vaccination is given through the nose.

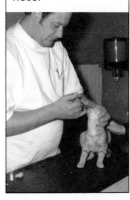

If your cat is entered for a show, it must be in tip-top condition and in perfect health.
It should have an especially good grooming before the show.

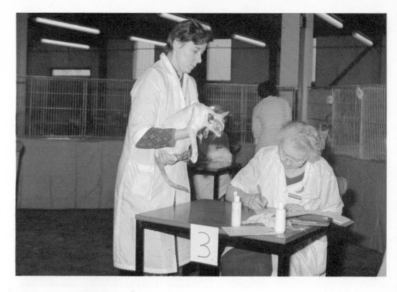

# Cat Shows

There are many cat shows held all over the country throughout the year.

Pedigreed cats have special shows.

There are different kinds of shows for pedigree cats.

For example, there are championship shows and less formal shows.

Many county shows and some of the larger pet shows have classes for non-pedigreed cats or household cats.

There are also shows for one breed of cat or several breeds.

Some of these may have a general pet section.

It is a good idea to visit some cat shows first if you are thinking about showing your own cat.
You will be able to see what they are like and perhaps talk to some of the people there.

You can find out about cat shows by looking in special cat magazines.

The largest cat show in the world is the National Cat Club's Show, held in London each year.

In the U.S.A., the biggest show is the Empire Cat Show in New York City.

All the cats entered for shows have to be examined by vets before they are allowed to compete.

Any cat that is ill or has fleas will be sent home.

Judges come round and look at cats in their show pens.

Each judge has a steward who will lift the cat out of its pen for the judge to examine.

There are many certificates, rosettes and trophies which can be won in each class. There is also a rosette or ribbon for the title of the Best Cat in the Show.

Whether you show your cat or not, whether your cat wins or not, you can have a lot of fun at a show. To you, your cat will always be the best there is!

# Checklist

**Before you get your cat:**

- Buy or make a bed (blanket).
- Buy three dishes or bowls.
- Buy enough food for the first few days.
- Buy or make a container to carry it home.
- Buy a litter tray.
- Check what food it eats, how much and how often.
- Check if it has had any vaccinations.
- Check if it has been wormed.
- Find out the name, address and telephone number of your nearest vet.
- Buy a cat collar with elastic inset if you wish.

---

**Each day:**

- Feed an adult cat twice a day, and kitten according to age.
- Water should be changed.
- Wash dishes after each meal.
- Groom with brush and comb.
- Remove soiled litter.
- Check for any signs of injury or illness.

**After the first week:**
- Take your cat to the vet to check that it is in good health.

**Each week:**
- Change and wash bedding.
- Throw away old cat litter.
- Wash and disinfect litter tray.
- Put fresh litter in the tray.

**At twelve weeks of age:**
- Take kitten to the vet to be vaccinated against cat flu and feline enteritis.

**At five months:**
- Neutering.

**Each year:**
- Take cat to vet for "booster" injections.

**When necessary:**
- Check for fleas.
- Check for worms.
- Take your cat to the vet to check that it is in good health.
- Have cat's claws clipped by the vet if you have no one to help you.
- Give cat special grooming for shows.

# Glossary

**Breed:** cats of the same type.

**Cat litter:** absorbent grains, shavings or peat put into the litter tray.

**Cross-bred:** cat which has parents of different breeds.

**Grooming:** brushing and combing the cat's coat to keep it in good condition.

**Kitten:** young cat up to about six months old. At cat shows a kitten is up to nine months old.

**Litter:** the name given to several kittens born to one female at the same time.

**Non-pedigreed:** cat which is of no special breed.

**Neutering:** small operation which stops female cats having kittens, and male cats from fathering kittens.

**Pedigreed (or pure-bred):** cat whose ancestors have been of the same breed for several generations.

**Quarantine:** separation of an animal from people and other animals for a time to stop possible spread of infection or illness.

**Rabies:** very infectious disease for all mammals.

**Weaning:** getting kittens used to solid food instead of their mother's milk.

# Index